THE PYRENEES
From the Pic du Midi d'Ossau to Comminges

Text written by Camille Fambon
Translated by
Ann MacDonald-Plénacoste

▲ *The Pyrenees. Behind the wooded hills towers the Pic du Midi de Bigorre, the remains of an ancient mountain dating from the primary era.*

◀ *Pyrenees bear, Musée de la Faune, Ayzac-Ost. This animal can weigh nearly 300 kilogrammes. It had almost disappeared, but it is now a protected species.*

▶ *The Ramonde (Ramondia Myconi). This typically Pyrenean flower is a cousin of the Cape Violet, a relic of the warm periods of the tertiary era.*

THE PYRENEES MOUNTAINS

Forty-five million years ago, a large island, the future Iberian peninsula, having broken away from Africa, collided with southern Eurasia. The Pyrenees were born out of this gigantic confrontation. Followed later by a general surrection, this genesis determined the structure of the range. An arm of the sea disappeared. The sediments covering its bed folded and formed to the north a calcareous rampart 1 000 to 2 000 metres high. Behind, old submerged massifs rose up to a height of over 3 000 metres: The Maladeta, and the Pic d'Aneto, the highest point in the Pyrenees (3 404 metres), the Luchonnais Mountains, the Néouvielle, the Cauterets-Panticosa massif, the Vignemale, the Balaïtous. The sedimentary coating with which the sea had covered them slid towards the south, creating a southern calcareous fringe exceeding 3 300 metres in the Gavarnie-Mont Perdu massif. Great rivers and then quaternary glaciers hewed out deep valleys perpendicular to the axis of the range: the high valley of the Garonne, the valley of Aure, the high valley of the Adour, the valley of the Gave de Pau (the Pau river), the valley of Ossau, the valley of Aspe. The Pyrenees are wild but humanised, with a mild, damp and yet sunny climate; the scenery is a delight to tourists, sportsmen appreciate the rambles and climbs, and naturalists enjoy the great variety of fauna and flora.

3

▲ *Ossau cheese. Made by the shepherds from pure ewes' milk, it is matured in salting tubs from which it emerges creamy and mild or dry and strong.*

▶ *One of the Ayous Lakes, Lake Gentau. It is one of a magnificent series of six mountain lakes, rising to a height of 2 000 metres.*

◀ *The Pic du Midi d'Ossau reflected in Lake Gentau. It is a huge block of lava, the remains of a volcanic mountain amphitheatre from the end of the primary era, broken up by the folding of the Pyrenees.*

▶ *The Pourtalet Pass. 1 794 metres high, between the valley of Ossau and the Spanish valley of Tena, it is the quickest way from Pau to Saragossa.*

▶ *Fabrèges Lake. It appears dominated in the west by the Chérue crests, the Saoubiste peak and the vertical block of the Pic du Midi d'Ossau.*

▶▶ *The little Artouste train. An overhead railway, high above the glacial valley of the Soussouéou and built for the requirements of a hydroelectric work-site, carries the train to Artouste Lake amid high mountain scenery.*

THE OSSAU VALLEY

The strange black silhouette of the Pic du Midi d'Ossau stands out due south of Pau. The superb valley of Ossau leads to it. The gateway is Arudy where the marble extracted from ancient coralline massifs is still worked. The first part of the glacial trough of the valley leaves room for two wide basins. Bielle, a museum village, is situated in the first. Former *capdhul* (county town), its beautiful traditional houses are often decorated with Renaissance windows taken from an abbey which was destroyed during the wars of Religion; it also has a charming Gothic church. Laruns is situated in the second basin. There the Valentin Valley joins up, dominated by the vertical walls of the Pic du Ger and leading to the spa resort of Eaux-Bonnes, very fashionable during the last century, and to the Gourette pastures criss-crossed with ski runs. Then the valley is hewn out into deep gorges where there is barely enough room for the spa resort of Eaux-Chaudes. It then emerges and leads to Gabas, a former shelter on the road to Compostelle, where it encounters the granite base of the Pic du Midi d'Ossau. Going around it to the easts, the valley runs along the Fabrèges artificial lake, departure point for a cable-car which ascends to Artouste and reaches the Pourtalet Pass. Another road, skiring the obstacle to the west, leads to Bious-Artigues Lake. Here it is possible to take a rough path to the admirable Ayous Lakes.

▲ *Aucun, a detail of the baptismal fonts. The Roman church of Aucun, modified during the 15th century, houses an 18th century altar piece and an altar front in Cordoue leather as well as a granite font and baptismal fonts encircled with crude sculptures evoking life in the Middle Ages (here a stone-cutter).*

◄ *Estaing Lake. This beautiful stretch of calm water lies at an altitude of 1 160 metres in a valley parallel to that of Arrens.*

▶ *The château de Beaucens. Formerly the property of the Viscounts of Lavedan, it is the largest mediaeval castle in the valley. It has been made into an ornithological park called the Donjon des Aigles (The Eagles' Keep) and has become famous for its impressive demonstrations of birds of prey in flight.*

TOWARDS THE LAVEDAN BY THE AUBISQUE PASS

In 1860, Napoleon III ordered the construction of spa roads to link up the important Pyrenean resorts. And the Empress exerted her influence so that the stretch be traced from Eaux-Bonnes, where she had taken the waters several times, to Argelès-Gazost via the Aubisque Pass. From this Pass, made famous by the Tour de France, the dangerous acrobatic overhanging road, high above the Cirque du Litor and its vast pastures, descends towards the Soulor Pass. The road then plunges down over gentle undulations, towards the valley of Arrens which it joins at the point where this valley, born in the severe surroundings of the Balaïtous, takes the name of the Val d'Azun. The Val d'Azun secretes an incomparable charm due to its long slopes and vast terraces facing south, to its villages solidly built of stone and slate grouped round beautiful mediaeval churches: Arrens, Aucun, Arras-en-Lavedan. On a terrace above the rich Argelès basin, crossed by the silver thread of the "Gave de Pau" (Pau river), the abbey-church of Saint-Savin is the only remaining but magnificent vestige of a very ancient and powerful monastic foundation dedicated to a 5th or 6th century hermit who lived in the nearby mountain. It was destroyed during the Revolution. Opposite, the two towers of the mediaeval castle of Beaucens rise up proudly.

▲▲ *The Cirque de Gourette, view from the Aubisque Pass. The ski resort (1 350 metres) nestles at the foot of the Pic du Ger (2 613 metres).*

▲ *The abbey church of Saint-Savin (12th century but the belfry dates from the 17th century). The interior, very dim, houses a beautiful 14th century Spanish Christ, a strange organ case and a mediaeval font known as that of the "cagots".*

The Egyptian percnopter, one of the birds at the Donjon les Aigles, is a white migratory vulture.

7

▶ *Massabielle Grotto. Bordered by the Gave, in 1858 it was known as the pigs' shelter.*

▲ *Bernadette Soubirous (1844-1879) portrait by Du Roure done in 1864. After the apparitions, Bernadette withdrew with the Sisters of Nevers where she died at the age of 35. A weak body but strong moral health.*

◀ *The basilicas. At the top, directly above the Grotto, the neogothic basilica of the Immaculate Conception (1871). Below it, the Rosary Basilica, dug out of the rock (1889).*

▶ *The Marian procession. It takes place every evening and is preceded every afternoon by the Eucharistic procession and the benediction of the sick.*

▶ *Lourdes castle. Apart from the keep which dates from 1407, it was rebuilt by Henri IV in 1590. Having lost all military value, it was a prison during the 18th century. Since 1920, it has housed the Pyrenean museum.*

▶▶ *The Bétharram caves. Fifteen kilometres west of Lourdes, under the Massif of the Toupiettes, 2 500 metres of galeries are open to the public. Electrically lit as early as 1902, they were the first caves to show tourists the marvels of the underground world.*

LOURDES, MARIAN CITY

In 1858, Lourdes was insignificant. Situated in a small basin at the entrance to the high valley of the Gave de Pau, it lived according to the rhythm of its castle, Cathare in 1216, English during the 100 Years War, at stake during the Wars of Religion. It was then made famous, quite unintentionally by a 14 year old girl, Bernadette Soubirous, daughter of a miller who had fallen into poverty. On February 11th, a very beautiful lady appeared to Bernadette in a vision in front of the Massabielle Grotto. The first fourteen apparitions – there were eighteen in all – provoked nothing but scepticism or even scandal; until that of March 25th 1858, when the Lady revealed her name "I am the Immaculate Conception". This was the beginning of a chain of events; inexplicable healings occurred. On January 18th 1862, His Grace Laurence declared: "The holy virgin really did appear to Bernadette". At the end of the century, the superposed Basilicas of the Rosary and the Immaculate Conception were built; in 1958, the gigantic underground Basilica of Saint Pius X was constructed; and in 1988, Saint Bernadette's church. Every day, between Easter and the Rosary pilgrimage, processions take place on the esplanade, the sick are bathed in the pools and a silent contemplative crowd gathers in front of the Grotto. Five million people visit Lourdes every year, including four hundred thousand sick people.

◀ *Cauterets. Nestled on a narrow shelf dominated by the Péguère peak, the old town is grouped around the church near the César thermal baths. In 1870 the town spread to the opposite bank of the Gave with a casino, magnificent villas and the luxurious Hôtel Continental and Hôtel d'Angleterre.*

▶ *Cauterets, the station. This picturesque wooden monument with its Far Wes look was the staion for an electric tramway which ran on an audacious railway built in 1897.*

▶ *The thermal baths and the Griffons waterfall. Recently enlarged, this establishment concerned with rhumatology is superbly situated between the Griffons and the Lutour waterfalls.*

▶▶ *Cauterets, César thermal baths. They were built in 1843 when water cures were highly fashionable. Other establishments developed during the second half of the 19th century: Pauze Vieux baths in 1853, the Œufs casino-thermal baths in 1869, the Neotherms in 1879...*

◀ *La Raillère. A "raillère" is a mass of fallen rocks. In this wild site, a commercial complex has developed alongside a reputed thermal establishment which, up unti the 1980's could be reached by means of a rack train.*

▶ *Ilhéou Lake. At an altitud. of nearly 2 000 metres, it lie. in a small basin between the crests separating it from the lovely valley of the Marcadau the ridges bordering the summit of the Grand Barba (2 800 m) and the Lys cirque where the downhill ski resort is being developed.*

CAUTERETS, THE REGION OF WATERFALLS

On the northern edge of a vast granite massif, three valleys converge towards a narrow steep-sided basin at an altitude of 900 metres. In the first valley, the little Gave d'Ilhéou, (Ilhéou river) emissary of Ilhéou Lake or the Blue Lake, tumbles down from the south-west. The second valley, running almost parallel to the first, is the Val de Jéret where the powerful Gave du Marcadau flows. The third is the Lutour Valley which plunges due south. Around this confluence, over twenty warm springs surge forth; this is why the place was called "Caldarrets", meaning the "boiler", origin of the name Cauterets. Today, harnessed and grouped together, these sodic sulphurated waters supply four large establishments dealing with rhumatology, dermatology, and ear, nose and throat treatment: the César thermal baths and those of the Rocher in Cauterets itself, La Raillère thermal baths and those of the Griffons a little further south. Some Gallo-Roman vestiges bear witness to the fact that certain springs have been known since ancient times.

In the 11th century, the Abbot of Saint-Savin, Lord of the valley, established baths. In 1316, he authorised the installation of a village in the basin of Cauterets, which remained occupied with pastoral activities even though it frequently welcomed very illustrious visitors, notably those belonging to the royal family of Navarre. The resort was only really brought

into fashion during the 18th century by Théophile de Bordeu, the famous doctor from the Béarn and the Maréchal de Richelieu. But Cauterets reached the height of its fame during the 19th century. A number of baths were modernised: César in 1836, Pauze in 1853, La Raillère in 1824, transformed and provided with its famous marble-columned pump room in 1888, the Casino des Œufs thermal baths in 1869. Beautiful dwellings with large marble-framed doors and windows replaced the tumbledown wooden cottages. Cauterets welcomed many guests of high repute: Queen Hortense, her husband Louis Bonaparte, the king of Holland, George Sand, Victor Hugo, Vigny… Around 1880, grand luxurious hotels were built for a rich international clientele. The two world wars brutally put an end to this expansion.

It resumed with the development of winter sports. The installation in 1963 of a cable car enabled the creation of the Lys downhill ski resort. Cross country skiing in the valley of the Marcadau followed around 1970. Today, there are several modern hotels and two thousand holiday homes. Because Cauterets is more than a resort. It is a whole region, hewn out of the granite, where the clear limpid mountain water flows in torrents, tumbles in waterfalls and ripples in more than fifty lakes within a range of deep valleys separated by high crests dominated by proud peaks.

▲ *Estom Lake. Beyond lies the high and difficult lake region of Estom-Soubiran.*

▶ *The Fruitière restaurant. At the outset of the Lutour Valley, it is the starting point for the walk to Estom Lake and the ascent of the Ardiden (2 988 metres).*

▶▶ *Boussès waterfall. Perhaps the most beautiful of the seven waterfalls in the Val de Jéret. In order to appreciate all its foaming splendour, it is necessary to walk up to the Pont d'Espagne (Spanish Bridge) by the path on its left bank.*

▲ *Cerisey waterfall. Situated at the side of the road which it sprays, this is the most admired waterfall in the Val de Jéret. Our ancestors liked to have their photographs taken there.*

▶ *The Pas de l'Ours (bear steps) waterfall upstream from the Cerisey waterfall. Alas, no bears have come this way for a long time…*

▲ Gaube Lake. During the Romantic period, people came here in sedan chairs.

The Vignemale, North face. The rock face, below the highest peak in the French Pyrenees (3 298 metres) has a vertical drop of 800 metres.

The Pont d'Espagne. Let there be no mistake! The border is a five-mile walk in the valley and the Port du Marcadau (Marcadau Pass) 2 566 metres.

The Pont d'Espagne waterfall.

THE PONT D'ESPAGNE

Upstream from the Val de Jéret, the road has to cross to the left bank by a stone bridge because of a heavy waterfall. For about a century now, this has been the *Pont d'Espagne* (Spanish Bridge). In earlier times, this was the name given to a rickety wooden bridge consisting of a few pine trunks thrown between two rocks a little further upstream. In fact, the Pont d'Espagne is a marvellous beauty spot enhanced by the converging waters from the Gaube Lake, which form the waterfall, and those of the Gave du Marcadau. The sight can be admired from the terraces of a hotel which was mentioned by the guide Joanne as early as 1868. The Pont d'Espagne is the gateway to two famous valleys. To the south-west, the superb valley of the Marcadau, (the Market) was thus named because the people of Cauterets and the Aragon people of Panticosa used to meet there to carry out their business deals! The valley has a series of rustic plateaux framed by wooded slopes separated by rocky shelves. It ends up at the Wallon refuge, the starting point for climbs and hikes to the great peaks and high passes of the border crest. Towards the south, the Gaube Valley, a typical example of a glacial valley, leads to the romantic Gaube Lake by an easy footpath; a more difficult path continues to the Oulettes de Gaube at the foot of the most formidable rock face in the Pyrenees: the North face of the Vignemale.

▲▲ The church of Luz. Called "the Templars' Church", it was in fact fortified by the Hospitaller Knights of Saint John of Jerusalem.

The Trinity. This strange painting exhibited in the museum of Luz church attempts to express the inexpressible mystery of one God in three Persons.

◀ The Pont Napoleon. It has a span of 42 metres.

▶ Bungee jumping. Adepts jump from a height of 70 metres above the torrent.

LUZ, SAINT-SAUVEUR AND NAPOLEON BRIDGE

Nestling at the confluence of the Bastan and the Gave de Gavarnie is the old part of the town of Luz with its slate-roofed houses huddled along narrow winding streets which converge towards the church of Saint-André, known as that of the Templars. Built around 1240, the Roman church is surrounded by rustic fortifications which were erected in 1340 to protect the populations from raids by brigands from Aragon. It has two entrances, one decorated with a sculpted tympanum and the other with 14th century frescoes. The interior, with a barrel vault, is austere. A chapel, added in 1664 during the plague, has been made into a museum. Opposite Luz stand the ruins of the Château Sainte-Marie built in the 13th century by the Counts of Bigorre. Further south, Saint-Sauveur, a small spa, lies on the opposite bank of the Gave de Gavarnie. This resort had its golden era during the Second Empire. The imperial couple came to Saint Sauveur during an official visit in 1859. Napoleon III had the church at Luz restored and a church built at Saint-Sauveur as well as the neighbouring chapel of Solferino. Above all, he ordered a bridge to be built extending the only street which, until then, had led only to the edge of a deep gorge. Building work began in the Spring of 1860 and the bridge was completed in August 1861. A road along the right bank was built later, making this admirable structure rather useless.

▲ *Gavarnie, the village and the Cirque.*

Gavarnie, the Hôtel des Voyageurs.

Gavarnie, the ascent to the Cirque. Gavarnie is the last place to have retained the tradition of rented mounts.

Gavarnie, the statue of Count Henry Russell Killough (1834-1909). This Irishman, born in Toulouse, haunted the Vignemale for years and had caves dug out as living quarters.

CIRQUE DE GAVARNIE

G avarnie! A myth, a miracle, according to Victor Hugo. The spot is phenomenal. A colossal mountain amphitheatre with superposed tiers, hewn out of a warm coloured sandstoney limestone stretching for three and a half kilometres at the foot and fourteen kilometres at the summit. All the summits which crown it are over three thousand metres high and are accentuated by glaciers. The end of the cirque, *l'oule* (the cooking pot) is austere but enhanced by countless flows of water including, above all, the Grande Cascade (the Great Waterfall) which plunges from a height of 423 metres; and thus the Gave de Pau is born. Paradoxically, this insurmountable obstacle lies next to an easily accessible pass perched at an altitude of 2 270 metres: the Col de Boucharo (Boucharo Pass), or the Port de Gavarnie (Gavarnie Pass). Even before 1150, an *hôpital* – that is a stopover shelter – was built on the site of the present village. In 1257, it was acquired by the Hospitaller knights of Saint John of Jerusalem, a religious order dedicated to the protection of pilgrims and travellers. Nothing remains of it today except perhaps the wooden statuette of Notre-Dame-du-Bon-Port (Our Lady of Safe Haven) who, with her right hand, offers a gourd to the pilgrim. In the 18th century rich tourists from the neighbouring spa resorts began to flock here. A early as 1740, an inn opened and later became the Hôtel des Voyageurs. It has welcomed all the

19

fathers of *Pyreneeism*: Ramond de Carbonnières, Packe, Russell, Saint Saud and many others. During the 1880's, Brulle, Bazillac, de Monts, led by a great dynasty of mountain guides, the Passet family, inaugurated the era of difficulty sought for its own sake, through what they pleasantly called, *les jeux du Cirque* (Cirque games). Today, even though it is easy to go to the Hôtel du Cirque at the threshold of the Oule by a good track on a rented horse, the upper tiers can still be reached only by rough paths. But the splendour of the scenery is beyond description. A trace in the mass of fallen rocks where the snow rises up to the Brèche de Roland, a titanesque gate opened over the desolate immensity of the Spanish sierras. The Pyrenees have five great cirques, a bouquet of gigantic corollas opened by the quaternary glaciers in thick layers of calcareous sediments. The most beautiful is unquestionably Gavarnie. The largest is that of Troumouse, the walls of which tower above its base from an average height of a thousand metres, stretching over a circumference of approximately ten kilometres. The smallest is Estaubé, access route to the massif of the Mont Perdu by the Breach of Tuquerouye (2 819 metres) from which point the mountaineer, like Ramond in 1796, discovers the north face of the Mont Perdu, the giant of the calcareous mountains (3 355 metres), ice clad, reflected in the ink blue of the Lac Glacé (Frozen Lake).

*Gavarnie, the Cirque.
its grandeur, its majesty,
its dimension are such that
the artists of the past had
great difficulty in setting it
on their canvasses. Perhaps
only the words of Victor
Hugo corresponds to the
impressions it inspires.*

◀ *The Brèche de Roland
(Roland's Breach). No-one
knows who gave this name
to the colossal opening one
hundred metres high and
forty metres wide perched at
an altitude of 2 800 metres.
In 1720, it was still known
as the Port du Haillou.*

▲ *The Cirque d'Estaubé.
In front of the snow cap on
the Mont Perdu, the Breach
de Tuquerouye appears.
In the foreground, the
southern extremity of the
Gloriettes artificial lake.*

◀◀ *The calcareous walls of
the Cirque de Troumouse.*

◀ *The Lac Glacé and the
north face of the Mont Perdu.
During the last century, the
glaciers formed a cascade
of seracs and died away in
the lake.*

◀ *The Col du Tourmalet (Tourmalet Pass), starting point of the road to the Pic, uses a passage in the crumbling shale between the Pic and the high granitic chain to the South.*

▶ *Barèges. Its thermal waters were famous as early as the 17th century as a remedy for bone injuries and illnesses. In 1775, the little Duke of Maine, son of Louis XIV was brought here by Madame de Maintenon as he suffered from a limp.*

▶ *The Pic du Midi de Bigorre. The* NASA *obtained the best photographs of the moon here for the preparation of the Apollo programme expeditions in 1969.*

▶▶ *La Mongie in winter. During the 12th century, the monks ("monges", hence the name La Mongie) were unable to subsist on its pastures. The 20th century saw the creation, on its snowfields linked to those of Barèges, of one of the largest ski domains in the Pyrenees.*

◀ *Bagnères-de-Bigorre. An old half-timbered house. Before the creation of the public thermal baths, the hot springs ran to beautiful private houses equipped with marble baths.*

▶ *The Médous caves. A few kilometres south of Bagnères-de-Bigorre, the Médous caves were discovered in 1948. They represent every possible type of concretion including the fine eccentrics going in every direction, unexplained until now.*

AROUND THE PIC DU MIDI DE BIGORRE

Standing out in the north of the chain with its towering summit 2 872 metres high, the Pic provides visitors with an immense panorama. The observatory which crowns it, built in 1878, was originally meteorological. But the air was so pure and so transparent that in 1907 work began on the installation of an astronomical observatory. Its two-metre mirror telescope was put into operation in 1980. Since 1962, the exceptional situation of the Pic has been exploited by a gigantic television antenna, 103 metres high, which serves the whole South-West. At the foot of the southern slope, the Col du Tourmalet (Tourmalet Pass) used to be the only access to Barèges. It became obsolete in 1744 following the completion of the road from Lourdes to Barèges but was rehabilitated during the second Empire by the creation of spa roads, the purpose of which was to link up all the spa resorts. This gave Barèges a considerable boost, and later the creation of the winter sports centre at La Mongie was made easier. In the north, the valley of Gripp, followed by that of Campan, ended at Bagnères-de-Bigorre, which was already a spa town in Roman times. Redesigned according to an urbanism plan in 1786, it was at its peak during the 19th century with the construction of the large thermal baths in 1823. Today it is still a spa but also an artistic, intellectual and scientific centre.

▲▲ *Arreau, the Maison des Lys. Hommage to the Crown of France to which the region was temporarily attached in 1512.*

▲ *Church of Jézeau, near Arreau. The Christ of the Last Judgement.*

▶ *Aragnouet. The Templars' chapel.*

◀ *The lake of Cap-de-Long and below it that of Orédon, raised by dams, constitute reserves of hydroelectric power and soften the severity of the landscape.*

▶ *The Néouvielle (3 091 metres). Even more than the severe granite walls, the countless lakes surrounded by pines constitute the incomparable charm of the massif and have justified its being classified as a nature reserve.*

SVPERBIA

▲ *Saint-Lary-Soulan. Saint Lary has become a large ski resort thanks to a cable car to the Pla d'Adet put into operation in 1957.*

Fresco from the church at Bourisp, near Saint-Lary. A cortège of women symbolises the seven deadly sins. Here, pride (end 16th century).

THE AURE VALLEY AND THE NÉOUVIELLE

To the east of the Pourtalet Pass, the high Pyrenean range seems to prevent all passage to Spain. South of Lannemezan, the rectilinear furrow of the Aure Valley provides a tempting solution. Initially wide and pleasant, it narrows at Sarrancolin crossing a strong calcareous bar where the veined red marble which decorates Versailles is still extracted. The valley then spreads out in the small bassin of Arreau at the confluence of the Neste d'Aure and the Neste du Louron. Arreau, which was once a modest capital, prospered from the 16th to the 19th century due to commerce and work in fine Spanish wool. It was the same for its neighbours, Ancizan, Guchen, Guchan, where beautiful houses with Renaissance windows can be seen. At the bottom of a long green basin, Saint-Lary, not content with its vast ski domain, has acquired ultra-modern thermal baths. Beyond, the valley becomes a gorge and curves to the west to skirt the massif of the Néouvielle. The road hesitates between several itineraries: the valley of the Rioumajou and the Ourdissétou Pass (2 403 metres), the valley of the Moudang, the small valley of the Géla and the Port Vieux (2 378 metres). It finally chooses the arrid valley de Saux and the Port de Bielsa perched at 2 429 metres. But is cheats with the mountain by piercing a three-kilometre long tunnel.

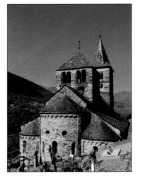

▲▲ *Fresco from the oratory of Mont, illustrating the life of Saint Catherine of Alexandria.*

▲ *Saint-Aventin, the church. Its features are the distinct architecture with two Lombard belfries and the quality of the sculpted decoration of its tympanum.*

▲ *Oô Lake. 40 hectares, 70 metres deep. The waters of Espingo Lake flow into it in a spectacular 273 metre-high waterfall.*

◀ *The winding road to the Peyresourde Pass rising above the valley of the Larboust.*

▶ *Espingo Lake. View towards the south from near the Espingo refuge. On the left, the Tusse de Montarqué. On the right, in the background, the Spijoles region (3 065 metres).*

BETWEEN THE VALLEYS OF AURE AND THE PIQUE

etween Arreau and Luchon, the Peyresourde Pass opens up a passage at an altitude of 1 569 metres, used by a road as early as the end of the 18th century. Firstly, the road follows the narrow valley of the Neste du Louron where Bordères-Louron, the only village, lies huddled. It then comes out into a huge 6 kilometre long basin, a hollow in which the Avajan and Génos-Loudenvielle Lakes are situated, edged with a line of villages flattened against the mountain to save the arable land. In spite of its isolation, this region has numerous Roman churches which were decorated with frescoes during the 15th and 16th centuries, the most remarkable being that of Mont, with its adjoining oratory. Beyond the Peyresourde Pass and the winter sports' resort, in the valley of the Larboust, the villages with their shining slate roofs cling to the sunny slopes, huddled around astonishing Roman churches: Cazeaux-de-Larboust, Castillon-de-Larboust, Saint-Aventin… To the south, the valley joins up with the Oô Valley which, by a stairway of lakes, rises towards a region described as *polar* during the last century: Lake Oô at 1 500 metres, lakes Espingo and Saussat at 1 900 metres and the Portillon Lake and the Lac Glacé at about 2 600 metres surrounded by magnificent summits.
In contrast, to the north, the Valley of Oueil is gently pastoral. And then the road plunges down to Bagnères-de-Luchon.

► The thermal baths.
The Chambert baths with
their famous colonnade were
inaugurated in 1857, the
Casino in 1860.

▲ The flower festival:
Celebrated on the last
Sunday in August, it began
in 1888 with an improvised
battle of flowers in front
of the Arnative café, a
fashionable meeting place.

► The Enfer waterfall
(Hell's waterfall). Draining
the waters of a cirque formed
by the crests of high peaks
reaching 3 116 metres at the
Crabioules, the Enfer stream
tumbles into the Lys Valley
in a multitude of waterfalls.
The neighbouring power
station is a reminder that
this region is a great supplier
of hydroelectric power.

▲ Bagnères-de-Luchon,
a general view. Behind the
belfry the foliage of the Allées
d'Étigny laid out by the
grand intendant to link the
thermal baths to the town.

► The Boums de Vénasque.
The boums are small lakes
set into a mineral landscape
below the Vénasque Pass.

►► Superbagnères. This
was the first ski resort in the
Pyrenees. In the background,
the Maladeta.

BAGNÈRES-DE-LUCHON

I n 1667, Monsieur de Froidour, supervisor of the forests under Louis XIV, rediscovered baths "excellent and sovereign, but very inconvenient" where the thermal baths of the antique Ilixon had once been situated. The resort did not become well known however until the end of the 18th century when the great Mégret d'Étigny, Intendant of Gascony, took some famous visitors there: Field-marshal de Richelieu, the beautiful Madame de Brionne, Talleyrand... Under the second Empire, Luchon had triumphant seasons. Lamartine, Napoleon III's young son, Taine, Flaubert, Dumas, Rostand, even Bismarck stayed there – as did the first Pyrenean mountaineers. Nowadays, with its new thermal baths built in 1973 and the *Vaporarium*, Luchon welcomes three thousand visitors each season. But in addition to its waters, the town is surrounded by marvellous beauty spots. Crowned with a huge hotel, the grassy slopes of Superbagnères dominate the perfect curve of the glacial valley of the Lys which encounters the foot of the Maupas on the powerful Enfer waterfall. Opposite, the valley of the Pique rises to the old building of the Hospice de France from which a path leads to the the Vénasque Pass at an altitude of 2 444 metres where the sparkling splendour of the Maladeta and Aneto glaciers are suddenly revealed – the roof of the Pyrenees.

▲▲ *Saint-Bertrand-de-Comminges. A 15th century house.*

▲ *Valcabrère, Saint-Just church. Who this noble lady and the priest were, is unknown.*

▶ *Saint-Bertrand-de-Comminges. General view. In the foreground, Saint-Just de Valcabrère.*

◀ *Saint-Bertrand-de-Comminges, the tympanum. A vestige of the Roman cathedral, it is doubly original: because of its subject, the adoration of the wise men and because it portrays Saint Bertrand before he was canonized.*

▶ *Saint-Bertrand-de-Comminges, detail of a stall. The patron bishop Jean de Mauléon presented the jube and the carved wood choir enclosure to his canons for Christmas Eve 1535; amongst the stalls, this fine subject of meditation: temptation.*

▲ *The cloister of Saint-Bertrand-de-Comminges.
This pillar portraying the
four evangelists replaces
one of the double columns
bearing the arcatures.*

◄ *Saint-Bertrand-de-Comminges, reliquary.
They are enshrined in the
Mausoleum, built in the
15th century by Bishop
Pierre de Foix.*

SAINT-BERTRAND-DE-COMMINGES

S outh of Montréjeau at the edge of the beautiful valley of the Garonne, surrounded by old houses, the Basilica of Saint-Bertrand-de-Comminges stands high, arrogant and dominating, its mass crushing somewhat the neighbouring Roman church of Saint-Just de Valcabrère. And yet, few cities have suffered so much throughout History. In ancient times there was a magnificient town flanked by a fortified oppidum founded by the Great Pompey in the year 72 B.C.. It was destroyed in 408 by the Vandals. Rebuilt, its oppidum was completely ruined in 585 after having chosen the wrong side in a dynastic quarrel between Merovingians. Around the year 1100, a Saint Bishop, Bertrand de l'Isle-Jourdain, rebuilt it from the ruins. He had the Roman cathedral of Saint Marie built and gave it a cloister open to the mountain panorama. In 1305, the Pope of Avignon, Clement V, former Bishop of Comminges, decided to replace the Roman vault by a Gothic vault, 55 metres long, starting 28 metres above the ground. His successors erected first a mausoleum and then a jube and a chancel in carved wood and finally a magnificent organ case. Unfortunately, during the Wars of Religion, the Huguenots conquered the town three times; they pillaged it and destroyed the Bishop's palace.
The revolution abolished the episcopal seat, reducing the ancient capital to a village of three hundred inhabitants.

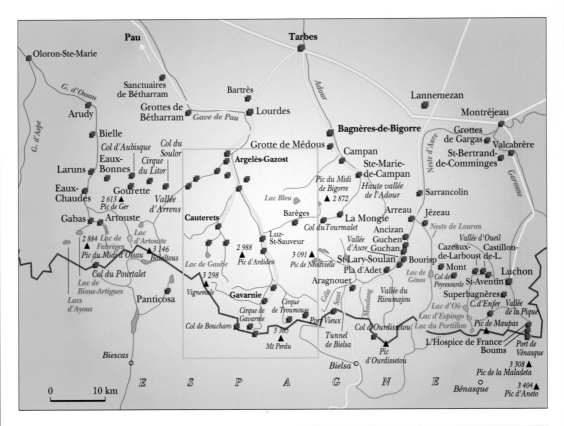

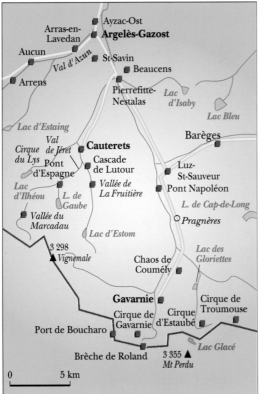

CONTENTS